AI-Powered Customer Service and Sales

How Smart Tools Are Revolutionizing Support, Speeding Up Sales, and Scaling Growth for Small Teams

Written by
Eric LeBouthillier

AcraSolution | 2025 1st Edition
www.acrasolution.com

Preface

Today's customers expect speed, personalization, and seamless support — but most small teams and solo founders don't have the time or tools to deliver all that manually.

That's where AI comes in.

This book is your shortcut to using AI tools — like ChatGPT, Intercom, and HubSpot — to automate customer service and sales in a way that's smart, efficient, and still human. You'll learn how to respond faster, follow up better, close more deals, and create systems that work 24/7 without burning you out.

Whether you're new to AI or ready to scale smarter, this guide gives you real-world tools, best practices, and a 30-day action plan to turn automation into growth.

Let's build something faster, friendlier, and far more effective — together.

— Eric LeBouthillier
Author & Cybersecurity Strategist

For permission requests or inquiries, contact the publisher through the website : www.acrasolution.com

LEGAL DISCLAIMER

This eBook is provided for informational purposes only and does not constitute legal, financial, or professional advice. The author and publisher have made every reasonable effort to ensure the accuracy and completeness of the information contained herein; however, neither assumes any responsibility for errors, omissions, or contrary interpretations of the subject matter.

Readers are encouraged to consult with qualified professionals for specific advice tailored to their individual needs. The mention of any products, services, or third-party entities does not imply an endorsement or guarantee of their effectiveness or suitability. Any application of the strategies and recommendations presented is at the reader's discretion and risk.

The author and publisher shall not be liable for any damages (including, without limitation, direct, indirect, incidental, or consequential) caused by the use, misuse, or interpretation of the information herein. All references to regulatory standards, statutes, or compliance requirements are informational and do not replace official legal counsel.

By reading and applying the concepts in this eBook, you acknowledge that you bear sole responsibility for the outcomes of your decisions and actions. If you do not agree to these terms, please discontinue use of this publication immediately.

Table of Contents

Who This Book Is For

This book is for anyone who wants to serve customers and close sales better, faster, and smarter — without a big team or technical background.

- **Solo founders, freelancers, and consultants** who want to automate busywork and free up more time to grow.
- **Small and medium business owners** looking to scale support and sales without hiring more staff.
- **Startup teams** who need to deliver 24/7 service and personalized experiences with limited resources.
- **Customer support managers and sales leaders** who want practical, step-by-step ways to use AI in their daily workflow.
- **Digital agencies and service providers** eager to offer smarter, more responsive service and win more business.
- **Anyone curious about AI** — and how it can make real, immediate impact in everyday business operations.

Whether you're just starting out or ready to level up your customer experience and sales process, this book is designed to give you real-world tools, clear strategies, and a proven 30-day action plan you can put to work right away.

Chapter 1: The AI Revolution in Customer Relationships

Introduction

Something profound has changed in how businesses connect with their customers—and it's not just technology. It's the shifting expectation that *every* interaction, whether it's a complaint or a question, a sale or a suggestion, should feel personal, fast, and frictionless.

For small and midsize businesses (SMBs), this used to be a near-impossible ask. Limited staff, disjointed tools, and siloed departments made seamless service feel out of reach. But today, artificial intelligence is redrawing the lines—and the rules—between support and sales.

The old boundaries no longer apply. AI doesn't just respond to problems; it anticipates them. It doesn't just close tickets; it opens conversations. And most importantly, it enables lean teams to deliver enterprise-level engagement at a fraction of the cost.

The Death of the Support Silo

In traditional businesses, support and sales operated like neighboring kingdoms—sharing a wall, but rarely a mission.

Sales focused on acquisition. Support dealt with complaints. And while both interacted with the same customers, their data, goals, and tools often lived in different systems. This "support silo" model not only slowed responses—it lost opportunities.

AI changes that dynamic entirely.

Modern AI-powered platforms unify support and sales into a single, continuous experience. Here's what that means in practice:

- A chatbot that resolves product questions *and* recommends upgrades
- A helpdesk that turns common complaints into upsell opportunities
- An AI assistant that remembers preferences across sessions, channels, and departments

By removing the handoffs, AI helps teams focus less on *who owns the interaction* and more on *what the customer needs next.*

Common Pitfalls of the Old Model:

- Repeating information to multiple agents
- Missed follow-up opportunities after a support interaction
- Lack of visibility into customer history across departments

Tactical Advantages of an AI-Unified Approach:

- Real-time sharing of customer context across sales and service
- Faster resolutions, fewer dropped leads
- Consistent tone and messaging from first click to final sale

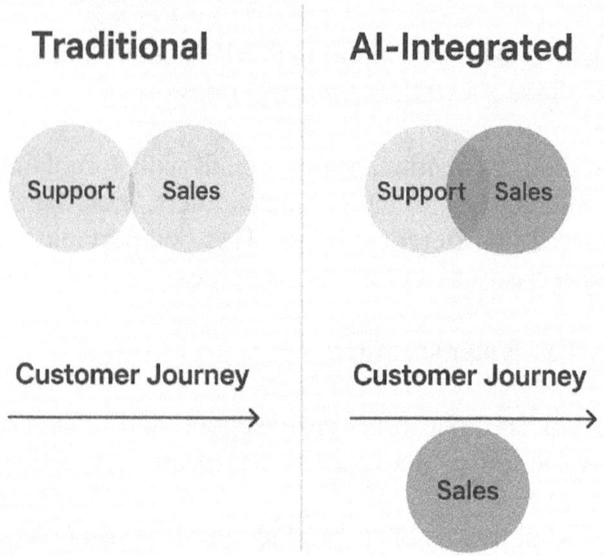

Summary:
This flowchart illustrates the shift from a traditional, siloed approach—where customer support and sales function separately—to a modern AI-integrated model. In the AI-powered journey, support and sales roles overlap, enabling faster responses, more personalized interactions, and a seamless customer experience across the entire lifecycle.

From Reactive Helpdesk to Proactive Relationship-Building

Historically, support teams were firefighters—reacting only when something went wrong. But today's AI doesn't wait for the phone to ring. It *initiates* the conversation, often long before the customer realizes they need help.

Consider these AI capabilities that shift the dynamic:

- **Predictive Suggestions**: AI can detect behavior patterns that indicate confusion or churn, and step in with offers or explanations
- **Conversational AI**: Tools like ChatGPT can engage users naturally and guide them through decisions or troubleshooting
- **Smart Routing**: Instead of queuing every inquiry, AI can resolve common requests instantly, or escalate only when needed

This shift isn't just about convenience—it builds trust. Customers feel seen, heard, and guided. And that transforms your support team from a cost center into a loyalty engine.

Proactive AI in Action:

- A customer pauses on the checkout page—AI offers live help or a promo code
- After a support issue is resolved, the AI follows up with a review request and product recommendation
- Based on browsing behavior, the AI notifies a rep to reach out with a custom quote

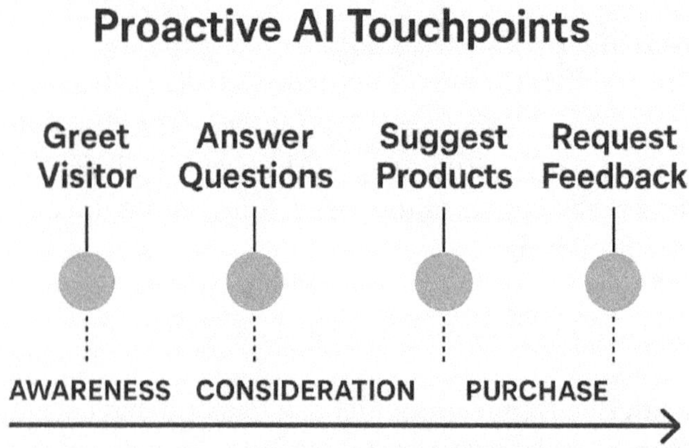

Proactive AI Touchpoints

Throughevar the cton-stepping

Summary:
This timeline illustrates key proactive AI touchpoints across the customer journey. From greeting visitors during the awareness stage to answering questions, recommending products, and gathering feedback post-purchase, AI can enhance every phase with timely, helpful, and personalized interactions — improving both customer experience and conversion outcomes.

Key Stats on AI Impact in Support and Sales

Still wondering if this shift is more than hype? Let's ground the vision in some concrete data. The AI evolution in customer experience isn't coming—it's already here.

- **80%** of customer interactions will be handled by AI without human intervention by 2027 (Gartner)
- **3x** faster response times for AI-augmented support teams compared to traditional setups (Zendesk Benchmark Report)
- **60%** of customers say they're more likely to purchase from companies that offer AI-powered assistance (Salesforce State of Service)
- **$11B+** is the estimated cost savings across customer support globally due to AI by 2030 (Juniper Research)

For SMBs, this means a chance to *do more with less*—and to compete on customer experience without ballooning headcount or tech debt.

Real-World Example: The Boutique Brand That Outgrew Its Inbox

What Happened:
A growing e-commerce brand selling specialty teas was drowning in customer messages—shipping updates, returns, product questions, and the occasional bulk order inquiry. Their small team couldn't keep up, and reviews started to reflect long response times.

What Went Wrong:
They were managing all communication manually through email. Sales and support were handled separately, and there was no shared view of the customer. One agent might be handling a complaint, while another was unaware that the same customer was also negotiating a wholesale deal.

What Changed:
The brand implemented an AI-driven support system (Tidio, paired with Shopify and HubSpot). Within days, their chatbot began resolving up to 65% of daily inquiries automatically. The system also flagged high-value customers for human follow-up, bridging the gap between support and sales.

What We Learn:
AI doesn't replace your team—it *amplifies* it. By clearing routine tasks and connecting customer data, even small teams can deliver big-brand service.

Conclusion

The line between support and sales is vanishing—and for good reason. Customers don't care which department they're talking to. They care about clarity, speed, and being understood.

AI helps SMBs deliver on those expectations, not just by reacting better, but by anticipating needs, personalizing journeys, and converting service into strategy.

The support silo is dead. In its place: a dynamic, AI-powered relationship engine that turns every touchpoint into an opportunity to impress and retain.

Next Steps

To make this shift work, you'll need the right tools—ones that are powerful, affordable, and built for teams like yours. In the next chapter, we'll break down the leading AI platforms that are transforming support and sales for startups, small teams, and agencies alike.

Chapter 2: Meet Your Digital Dream Team (Top AI Tools)

Introduction

There's never been a better time to be a small business with big ambitions. Thanks to a wave of intelligent, affordable AI platforms, SMBs now have access to the same cutting-edge capabilities once reserved for enterprise giants — without the cost or complexity.

From automating responses and routing leads to nurturing prospects and resolving support tickets, today's AI tools can help your business do *more* with *less*. But not all tools are created equal, and not every one is right for your size, budget, or workflow.

This chapter introduces the essential players in your digital dream team — the top AI platforms that power smarter customer service and scalable sales without hiring a full-time army.

The Core AI Categories That Matter

Before diving into specific tools, it helps to understand the core functions they cover. Most of the platforms in this chapter fall into one or more of these categories:

- **Conversational AI** – Chatbots and virtual assistants that handle customer queries in real time
- **AI Helpdesk Automation** – Tools that triage, tag, and resolve support tickets using machine learning
- **CRM Intelligence** – AI that enhances customer relationship management with lead scoring, personalization, and predictive insights
- **Workflow Automation** – Tools that connect actions across your marketing, sales, and support stack

Each of the tools we cover below plays in one or more of these arenas — and together, they can completely transform your customer operations.

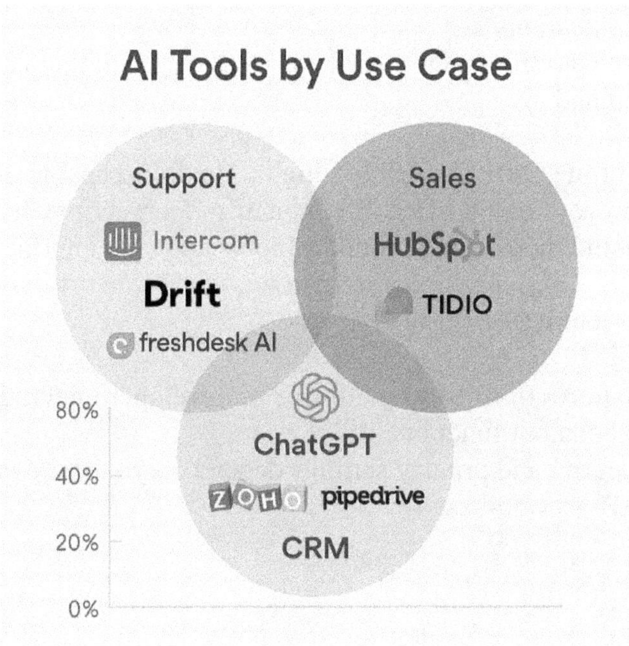

Summary:
This visual map categorizes top AI tools by business function — Support, Sales, and CRM — helping users quickly identify which platforms serve which purpose. Tools like Intercom, Drift, and Freshdesk AI support customer interactions, while HubSpot and Tidio drive sales. CRM platforms such as Zoho and Pipedrive manage pipeline and customer data, with ChatGPT overlapping all three categories as a flexible, general-purpose AI assistant.

Tool 1: ChatGPT (OpenAI)

Best for: Dynamic conversations, content generation, and scalable customer engagement

Use Cases:

- Powering custom chatbots for support and sales
- Writing personalized replies, email responses, and product explanations
- Brainstorming new campaign ideas or generating content on demand

Why It Stands Out: ChatGPT is highly flexible, capable of adapting to your brand voice, FAQs, and support scripts. It's the engine behind many custom-built AI tools and chat interfaces.

Things to Know:

- Requires third-party platforms or developer integration for full chatbot functionality
- Security and privacy settings depend on your implementation (API vs web-based)

Tool 2: Intercom

Best for: Growing teams that want an all-in-one solution for customer messaging and support

Use Cases:

- Live chat + AI agent hybrid model
- Proactive engagement based on user behavior
- Support ticket deflection and automated answers

Why It Stands Out: Intercom blends AI-powered bots with human support in one dashboard. It's designed for scaling teams that want to engage intelligently and reduce ticket volume.

Things to Know:

- Pricing scales quickly with usage
- Best suited for SaaS, B2B, and product-led companies

Tool 3: Freshdesk AI (by Freshworks)

Best for: Service-heavy SMBs that need robust ticketing with AI built in

Use Cases:

- Automated ticket classification and routing
- AI-assisted responses for agents
- Real-time sentiment analysis

Why It Stands Out: Freshdesk's AI (called Freddy) helps teams streamline support operations with practical automations that don't require custom code.

Things to Know:

- Strong support features, but less sales automation
- Works best when paired with other Freshworks products

Tool 4: HubSpot AI

Best for: Businesses already using HubSpot for marketing, sales, or CRM

Use Cases:

- Lead scoring and prioritization
- Predictive deal insights
- AI-generated email suggestions and chatbots

Why It Stands Out: HubSpot AI is deeply embedded in an already powerful ecosystem. It's ideal for businesses that want automation across the full customer lifecycle, from lead gen to retention.

Things to Know:

- Requires a paid HubSpot plan
- Works best when fully integrated across marketing and sales

---

Tool 5: Drift

Best for: B2B companies focused on conversational selling

Use Cases:

- Qualifying leads through chatbot conversations
- Routing high-value prospects to sales instantly
- Personalized engagement for repeat visitors

Why It Stands Out: Drift pioneered "conversational marketing" — using bots not just to support, but to sell. It's tailored for high-intent, complex buyer journeys.

Things to Know:

- Geared toward mid-market and enterprise pricing
- Strong sales alignment, less focus on support workflows

Tool 6: Tidio

Best for: E-commerce and lean teams wanting quick wins with minimal setup

Use Cases:

- Automating FAQ responses and order tracking
- Combining live chat with AI-powered answers
- Email and Messenger integration for multichannel coverage

Why It Stands Out: Tidio is lightweight, fast to deploy, and surprisingly powerful. It's built for SMBs that need instant automation without complexity.

Things to Know:

- Ideal for Shopify and WooCommerce integrations
- Limited CRM capabilities compared to others

Quick Comparison Table

Tool	Complexity	Cost Range	Best Fit	Standout Features
ChatGPT	Medium	$20–$200+	Custom setups, content tasks	Natural language generation
Intercom	High	$$$	SaaS, product support	Hybrid support + behavior targeting
Freshdesk	Medium	$$	Service-focused SMBs	Ticket automation + sentiment tracking
HubSpot AI	Medium	$$–$$$	CRM-driven teams	AI email, lead scoring
Drift	High	$$$$	B2B sales orgs	Conversational selling
Tidio	Low	$–$$	E-commerce, small teams	Plug-and-play chatbot with live chat

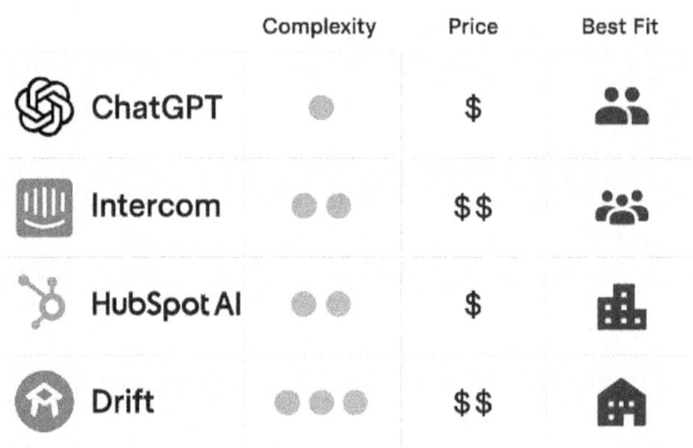

Summary:
This visual comparison chart highlights four leading AI tools—ChatGPT, Intercom, HubSpot AI, and Drift—across three key factors: complexity, price, and best fit. It helps readers quickly assess which platform aligns with their needs, whether they're a solo founder, small team, or growing business. The layout offers a clean, intuitive guide for choosing the right AI solution without overwhelming the decision-making process.

Tactical Best Practices for Choosing Your AI Stack:

- Match the tool to your *team's capacity*, not just your vision
- Look for integration with your existing platforms (Shopify, CRM, etc.)
- Start with one primary tool before adding more — avoid tool sprawl

Common Mistakes SMBs Make:

- Paying for enterprise-level features they never use
- Choosing tools with steep learning curves and no internal champion
- Overlooking customer data flow between tools

Real-World Example: From Overwhelmed Inboxes to an Always-On Sales Engine

What Happened:
A small digital marketing agency was spending hours each week answering the same pre-sale questions: pricing, packages, turnaround time. Despite having a talented team, they couldn't scale outreach without dropping the ball on leads.

What Went Right:
They implemented Drift and trained the AI bot to qualify leads based on budget and need. High-value prospects were routed to the founder directly. FAQs were answered instantly, and conversations continued via email when needed.

Results:
Within two weeks, they cut lead response time from 36 hours to 4 minutes — and closed three new contracts just from automated engagement.

Key Takeaway:
With the right AI tool, even a tiny team can *look* and *operate* like a much larger one — without hiring or burning out.

Summary:
This workflow diagram shows how a small business team can use AI tools across daily operations. A chatbot handles incoming inquiries, the CRM automatically scores leads, and AI-driven systems send personalized follow-up emails — creating a seamless, efficient pipeline across sales, marketing, and support with minimal manual effort.

Conclusion

Your digital dream team isn't made of employees — it's made of *smart systems* working in sync. With the right AI tools in place, small businesses can compete on speed, service, and personalization like never before.

Start small, choose strategically, and build your stack around what *actually* saves time and generates results.

Next Steps

Now that you've met the core tools, it's time to put them to work — starting with the frontline. In the next chapter, we'll dive into **AI-powered chatbots** that can handle up to 80% of customer questions — without making the experience feel robotic.

Chapter 3: Automate the Frontline — Chatbots That Actually Help

Introduction

Customers today expect instant answers — but they still want to feel understood. That's the core challenge at the frontline of service: how to scale speed without losing the human touch. The answer? Conversational AI that's actually helpful.

Modern AI chatbots have matured far beyond the clunky scripts of the past. With natural language processing, FAQ integration, multilingual capabilities, and seamless escalation paths, today's bots can handle **80% or more** of customer inquiries — freeing up your team for the edge cases that require a human brain.

Done right, chatbots don't just deflect tickets — they build trust, convert leads, and provide 24/7 value to your customers. But execution matters. This chapter is your tactical guide to doing it right.

Bot vs Human: Designing a Smart Handoff Flow

A great chatbot doesn't pretend to be human — it knows when *to call one in.*

The best systems are built on a clear handoff logic: when to escalate, who to route to, and how to do it *without frustrating the customer*. A smooth transition between bot and human support is the difference between a seamless experience and a service fail.

Smart handoff flows typically include:

- Trigger thresholds (e.g., number of failed bot responses)
- Customer sentiment analysis (anger, confusion)
- Direct escalation keywords (e.g., "agent," "talk to someone")

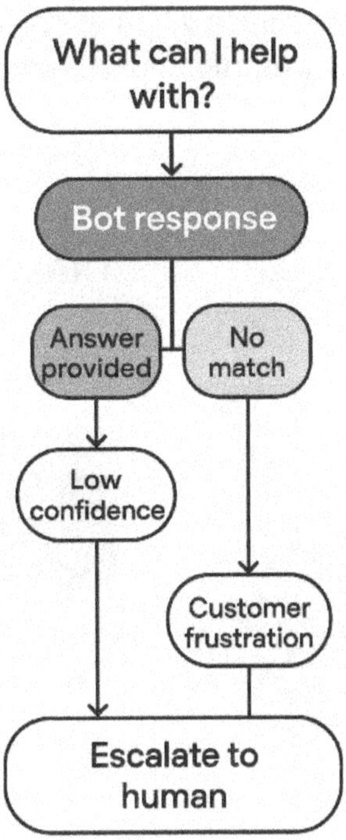

Pre-Training with Real FAQs

The biggest reason chatbots fail? They don't know your business.

A bot trained on generic answers will frustrate your customers. But one trained on **your actual FAQs**, **support tickets**, and **live chat logs** will feel like it's been with your company for years.

Key content sources for training your bot:

- Past support transcripts (look for common issues and keywords)
- Knowledge base articles and help docs
- Sales questions from your contact forms or email inquiries

Best Practices:

- Structure answers with clarity (think one idea per message)
- Link to deeper resources when appropriate
- Regularly update training data as new patterns emerge

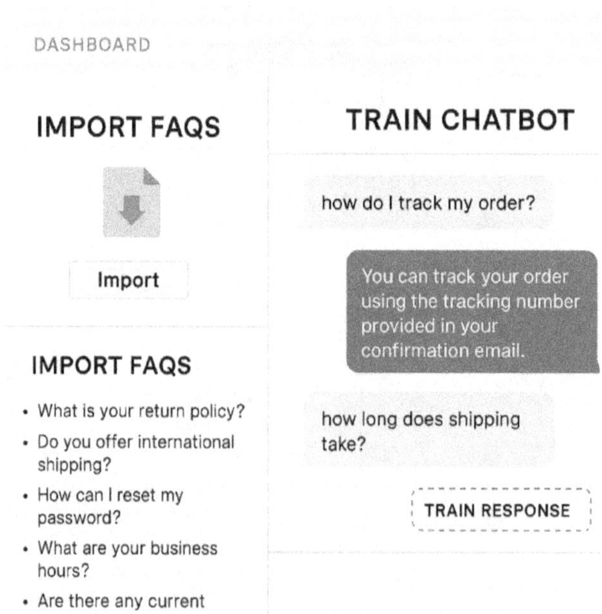

Multilingual Support Without Multilingual Teams

Your customers may come from different countries — your support team doesn't have to.

Thanks to AI-powered translation, today's leading chatbot platforms can handle **dozens of languages** automatically. The customer types in French, your bot responds in French — even if your original content is in English.

Key Capabilities to Look For:

- Auto-translation based on detected input language
- Ability to train the bot on multiple language variants
- Seamless language switching mid-conversation

Ideal For:

- E-commerce stores with international customers
- SaaS companies with global user bases
- Travel, hospitality, or services targeting multilingual markets

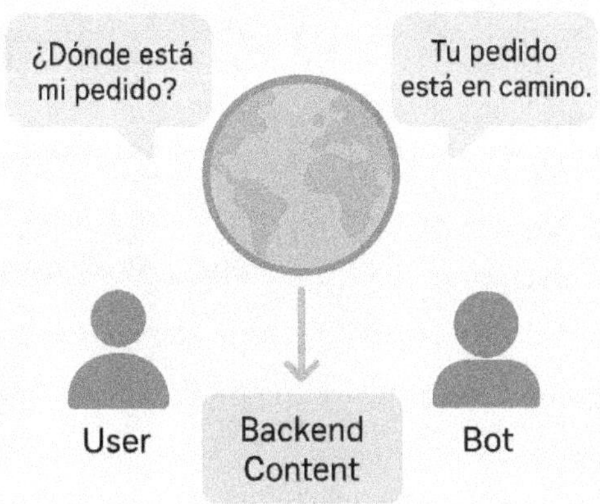

Do's and Don'ts for Chatbot Implementation

Not all bots succeed. The difference often comes down to how they're implemented and maintained. Here are some quick do's and don'ts:

Do:

- Pre-load the bot with real-world data from your business
- Make it easy for users to request a human at any time
- Keep language simple, natural, and on-brand
- Test weekly and refine based on transcript reviews

Don't:

- Overpromise the bot's capabilities ("Ask me anything!")
- Force customers to navigate rigid menus
- Leave escalation paths unclear
- Forget to update it as your business evolves

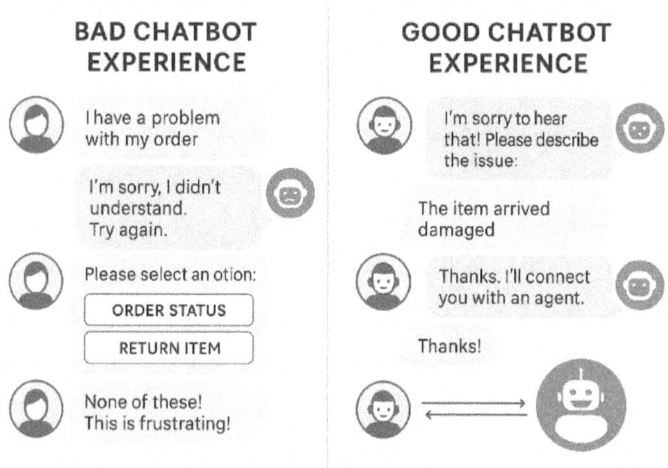

Real-World Example: From Support Drain to Sales Driver

What Happened:
A mid-sized subscription box company was struggling with over 400 repetitive support tickets a week — order tracking, billing questions, and product confusion. Their 3-person team was overwhelmed, and customers were frustrated by long wait times.

The Fix:
They deployed an AI chatbot through Intercom, trained it on their top 25 FAQs, and programmed it to escalate complex questions after 2 failed attempts. It also greeted customers with proactive order lookups based on email.

The Results:
Within 30 days, bot-handled inquiries jumped to 76%. Customer satisfaction rose 18 points. Even better — the bot began answering pre-sale questions and directing visitors to pricing pages, contributing to a 12% bump in conversions.

Lesson:
A well-trained, well-placed chatbot does more than reduce workload — it drives revenue.

Conclusion

Chatbots are no longer a novelty — they're a frontline necessity. When designed with care and powered by AI, they provide *speed*, *scale*, and *satisfaction*. For SMBs, they're not just helpful — they're transformational.

But remember: the goal isn't to *replace* humans. It's to elevate them — by letting AI handle the predictable, and people handle the personal.

Next Steps

In the next chapter, we explore how AI can *extend* your service coverage beyond business hours — including auto-routing, escalation, and intelligent triage systems that ensure no customer is ever left waiting.

Chapter 4: 24/7 Service Without the Overhead

Introduction

The days of "business hours only" support are over. Customers expect responses around the clock — even at 2 a.m. on a Sunday. But for most small and midsize businesses, staffing a 24/7 team simply isn't realistic.

This is where AI delivers its greatest advantage: constant availability without constant overhead.

AI doesn't sleep, doesn't get tired, and doesn't go on vacation. Whether it's routing a ticket, calming a frustrated customer, or answering a late-night question via voice assistant, today's tools make it possible to serve customers instantly — without hiring more people.

Auto-Routing Tickets to the Right Place

One of the fastest ways to reduce response time — and improve satisfaction — is to make sure every inquiry lands in the *right* place, *right away.*

AI can scan incoming messages, detect intent, urgency, and even category, then route tickets based on logic and business rules.

Smart Routing Includes:

- Prioritizing urgent issues (e.g., "order not received")
- Assigning technical queries to the right team
- Flagging VIP or high-spend customers for priority handling

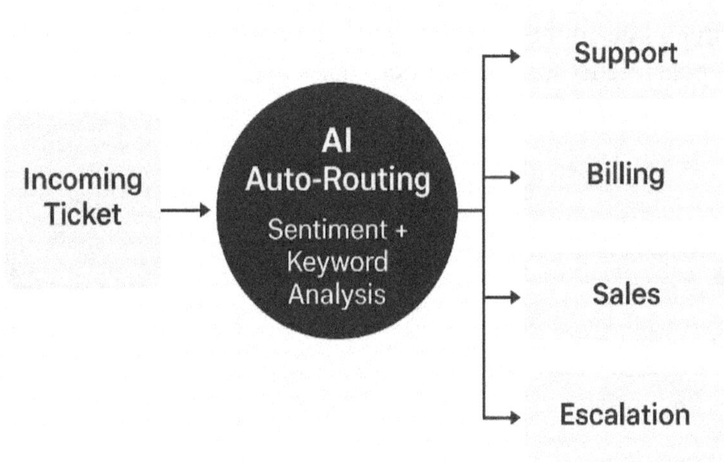

Sentiment Analysis and Escalation Triggers

What if your AI could tell when a customer was *angry*, *confused*, or *ready to cancel* — and respond before things spiral?

AI sentiment analysis tracks language patterns, tone, and behavior to detect emotional signals. When it senses distress or urgency, it can automatically alert a human, upgrade the ticket, or escalate the case in real-time.

Common Escalation Triggers:

- Negative sentiment (e.g., "this is ridiculous," "I'm done waiting")
- High-value account + unresolved complaint
- Multiple contact attempts in a short window

Benefits for SMBs:

- Protects reputation by catching issues early
- Saves high-value accounts from churn
- Empowers agents with real context before jumping in

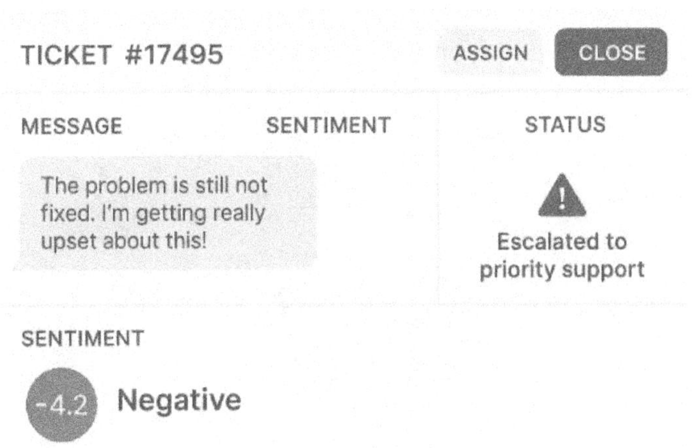

Voice Assistant Integrations

Not every customer wants to type. Increasingly, they're using voice — through phones, smart speakers, and in-app voice AI — to get what they need.

Platforms like Alexa for Business, Google Dialogflow, and custom voicebots let you create natural spoken interfaces for common service needs.

Real-World Voice Use Cases:

- "Check the status of my order" via smart speaker
- Booking an appointment or callback without opening a website
- Troubleshooting a product issue hands-free

Voice AI can:

- Answer and resolve routine calls without agent intervention
- Integrate with CRMs and knowledge bases
- Capture intent and direct customers to the right next step

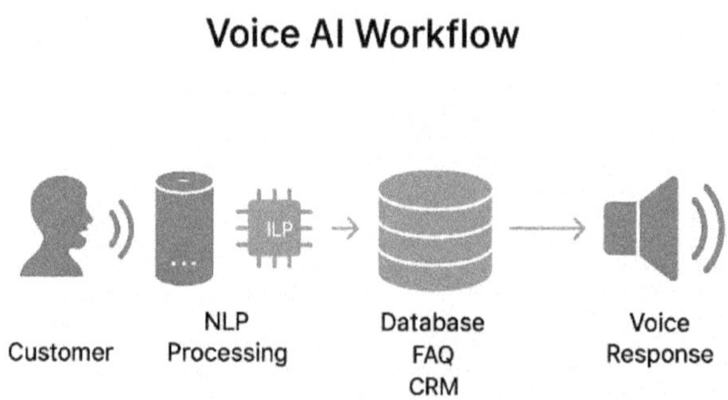

Voice AI Workflow

Summary:
This schematic illustrates a Voice AI workflow, beginning with a customer speaking to a smart device. The request is processed by a natural language processing (NLP) engine, which queries data from an FAQ or CRM database. A relevant voice response is then generated and returned to the customer, showcasing a seamless loop of AI-powered voice interaction.

Building Your "First Response" AI Layer

Think of your first response layer as the *digital concierge* that greets every customer, triages their needs, and makes sure they're either helped instantly or escalated appropriately.

It's not just a chatbot — it's a full system designed to intercept, classify, and handle the majority of inbound inquiries *without* waiting on a human.

A Strong First Response Layer Should:

- Acknowledge the customer instantly ("We've got your request")
- Provide relevant self-help or direct answers
- Escalate when needed — without delay or confusion
- Log and route the conversation seamlessly

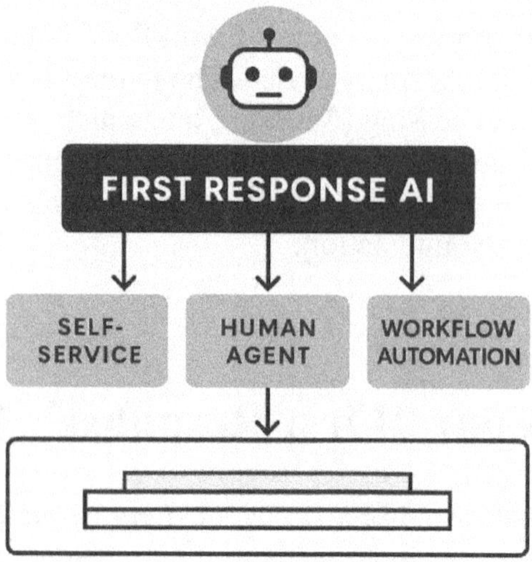

Summary:
This layered architecture diagram illustrates how First Response AI acts as the front line in customer service, instantly handling incoming requests. From there, it routes the interaction to one of three destinations: self-service for simple tasks, a human agent for complex issues, or workflow automation for behind-the-scenes processes—ensuring efficient, intelligent support from the first touchpoint.

Real-World Example: The Clinic That Never Missed a Call

What Happened:
A wellness clinic offering therapy and coaching was losing potential clients after-hours. Many inquiries came in at night, when no one was available to answer — leading to frustration, lost bookings, and negative reviews.

The Fix:
They implemented a voice-enabled AI assistant that could answer calls, identify intent (booking vs. info vs. cancellation), and schedule appointments directly in their calendar. Sentiment analysis was added to alert staff if someone sounded distressed or angry.

Results:
They reduced missed calls by 78%, booked 40% more appointments outside business hours, and identified two serious support issues before they escalated into legal complaints.

Key Takeaway:
AI isn't just about faster service — it's about *never missing a moment* to help or protect your customer.

Conclusion

AI-powered 24/7 service isn't just a convenience — it's a competitive advantage. For SMBs, it levels the playing field against bigger players with round-the-clock staffing. With the right setup, you can provide immediate, intelligent, and emotionally aware service at any hour.

Let AI take the night shift, so your team can focus on impact, not interruptions.

Next Steps

Now that your support layer is operating around the clock, it's time to bring the same intelligence to your **sales funnel**. In the next chapter, we'll explore how AI turns curious visitors into loyal buyers — with personalized replies, lead scoring, and automated follow-ups.

Chapter 5: AI in Sales — From Leads to Loyalty

Introduction

Sales used to be a numbers game — more calls, more emails, more follow-ups. But AI is flipping that model. Today, it's not about *doing more*, it's about *doing it smarter*.

With AI, SMBs can deliver personalized experiences, anticipate buyer intent, and follow up with perfect timing — all without hiring a bigger team. From auto-generated email replies to precision-targeted upsells, modern sales AI tools are helping businesses turn browsers into buyers, and one-time customers into loyal advocates.

Let's break down how to use AI across your entire sales funnel — from the first click to the final conversion.

GPT-Powered Email Replies That Feel Personal

Whether it's answering product questions, following up after a demo, or nurturing a cold lead, email is still one of the most powerful tools in your sales toolbox — and AI makes it smarter.

AI language models like ChatGPT can now generate or assist in writing **natural, on-brand, and relevant** sales emails in seconds. Trained on your product info, buyer personas, and tone of voice, they can create replies that feel personal — without the manual effort.

Use Cases:

- Responding to inquiries with dynamic product recommendations
- Drafting follow-ups tailored to user behavior
- Polishing outreach emails that sound human, not robotic

Best Practices:

- Use templated prompts for consistent structure
- Always review/edit before sending — tone still matters
- Personalize the opener and closer for key accounts

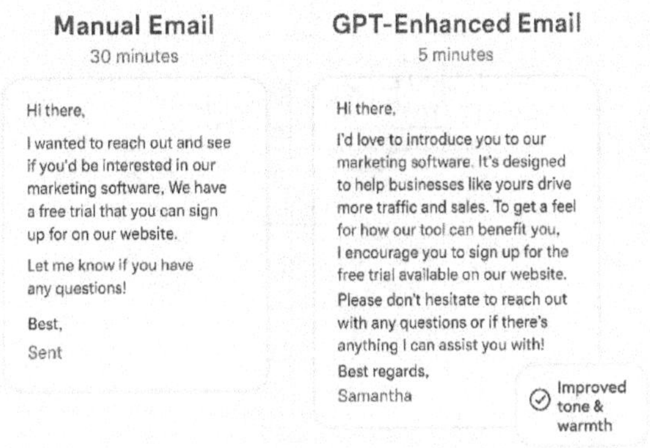

Lead Scoring with CRM + AI

Not all leads are created equal. AI can analyze lead behavior — clicks, opens, time on site, interaction history — and score each one based on how likely they are to convert. This turns your sales strategy from *spray and pray* into *target and close*.

How It Works:

- AI models track signals like engagement level, company size, past purchases
- Each lead is given a score (0–100) based on likelihood to convert
- High-priority leads are flagged for immediate follow-up

Key Platforms:

- HubSpot AI Lead Scoring
- Zoho CRM Zia Insights
- Pipedrive Smart Contact Data

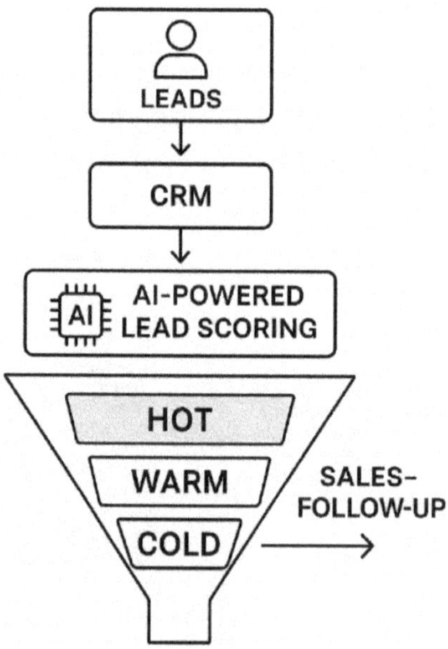

Automated Calendar Booking Flows

How much time do you lose going back and forth trying to book a meeting?

AI can handle that too. Tools like Calendly, Chili Piper, and HubSpot Meetings use AI logic to suggest optimal times, route bookings to the right sales rep, and trigger follow-up workflows — all without human input.

Features to Look For:

- Dynamic scheduling based on timezone, team availability
- AI-based meeting routing by territory or lead score
- Auto-confirmation and reminders via email or SMS

Benefits:

- Faster time to meeting = faster time to deal
- Fewer drop-offs due to missed replies
- More calendar fills with less coordination

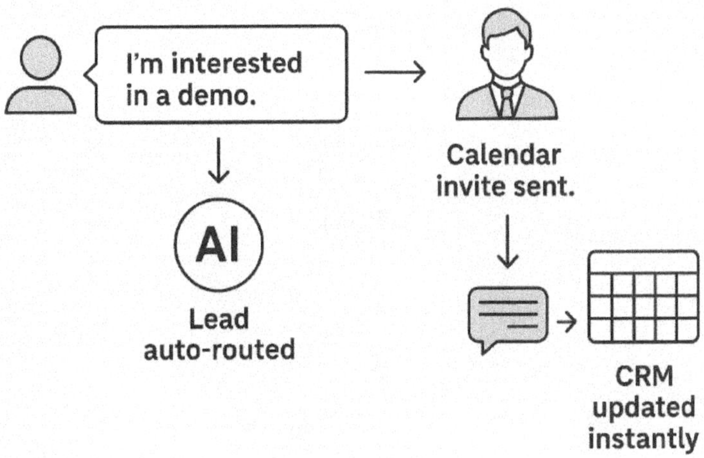

Personalized Upsell and Cross-Sell Logic

The best time to sell again? *Right after the first sale.* AI can identify what your customer is most likely to need next — and surface that recommendation at the perfect time.

By analyzing purchase history, usage patterns, and similar customer journeys, AI helps you offer products or upgrades that feel helpful, not pushy.

Examples:

- Recommending a higher-tier subscription based on feature usage
- Offering related accessories after a physical product sale
- Nudging a discount for reorders before renewal

Where This Works Best:

- E-commerce platforms like Shopify + Rebuy or LimeSpot
- SaaS platforms using Segment + AI personalization engines
- CRM-integrated upsell flows (HubSpot, Salesforce)

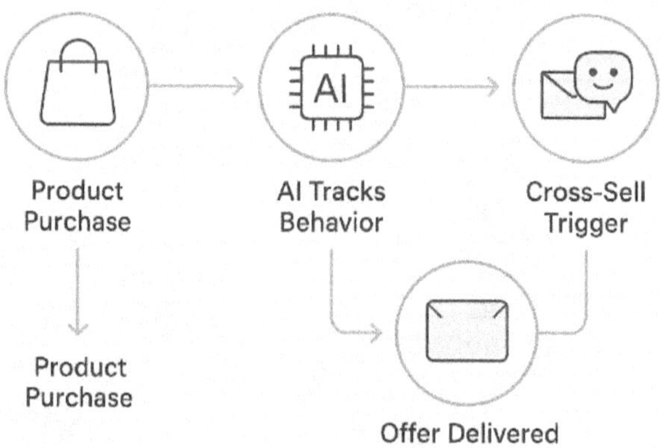

Real-World Example: From Cold Leads to Warm Closes

What Happened:
A boutique SaaS startup was sitting on 800+ stale leads from previous campaigns. They didn't have the staff to re-engage everyone manually, and their sales team was focused on active pipeline only.

What Changed:
They implemented GPT-assisted outreach using HubSpot AI to craft tailored reactivation emails. Leads who clicked were scored using AI based on past behavior, then routed to the right rep with calendar links embedded.

The Results:
Within 3 weeks, they reactivated 140 leads, booked 45 demos, and closed 12 new accounts — all without adding a single new salesperson.

Lesson:
AI in sales isn't just about automation. It's about making every interaction smarter, faster, and more likely to convert.

Conclusion

Sales success no longer depends on how many calls your team makes — it depends on how well your systems work together. AI bridges the gaps, removes the bottlenecks, and gives your team more time to focus on closing deals.

From smart replies to intelligent upsells, AI helps you meet the right customer, with the right message, at the right time.

Next Steps

In Chapter 6, we'll zoom in on the **CRM systems themselves** — the place where all your sales data lives. Learn how AI-powered CRMs turn your sales playbook into a smart, proactive engine that closes deals faster and more consistently.

Chapter 6: AI-Powered CRM — Your Sales Team's Brain Upgrade

Introduction

Your sales team is only as strong as the system behind them. And that system — your CRM — has just gotten a serious brain upgrade.

AI-powered CRMs are no longer just digital filing cabinets. They're intelligent assistants that help your team prioritize leads, customize messaging, suggest next steps, and even write proposals — all in real time. For small and midsize businesses, this means your CRM doesn't just track deals… it helps *close* them.

Let's explore how top CRMs like **HubSpot**, **Pipedrive**, and **Zoho AI** are transforming how sales teams work — with predictive intelligence, automated content, and razor-sharp deal insight.

Smart CRM Tools in Action: HubSpot, Pipedrive, Zoho AI

Each of these platforms has layered in AI to supercharge traditional CRM features:

HubSpot AI

- Predicts which deals are most likely to close
- Offers email writing assistance with tone suggestions
- Recommends next best actions based on buyer behavior

Pipedrive Smart AI

- Offers insights on deal momentum and performance trends
- Scores leads automatically and flags at-risk deals
- Surfaces visual forecasts for revenue and pipeline health

Zoho Zia AI

- Uses past data to suggest sales activities
- Generates intelligent alerts (e.g., "likely to churn")
- Helps write email follow-ups and log calls with one click

HubSpot	pipedrive	ZOHO
Predictive Lead Scoring	✓	✓
AI Insights	✓	✓
Automated Workflows	✓	✓
Content Assistance	✓	✓

Predictive Insights + Nudges That Drive Results

Predictive AI isn't about replacing intuition — it's about *informing* it.

Instead of combing through every opportunity manually, your CRM can now proactively alert reps to:

- Hot leads that need immediate follow-up
- Stalled deals that are at risk
- Surprising new opportunities based on behavior triggers

These AI "nudges" can be lifesavers in a busy day — and they often reveal trends humans would miss.

Examples of Nudges:

- "This deal is aging — send a follow-up?"
- "Customer opened your last three emails — time to call?"
- "Prospect viewed pricing page twice — suggest scheduling a demo"

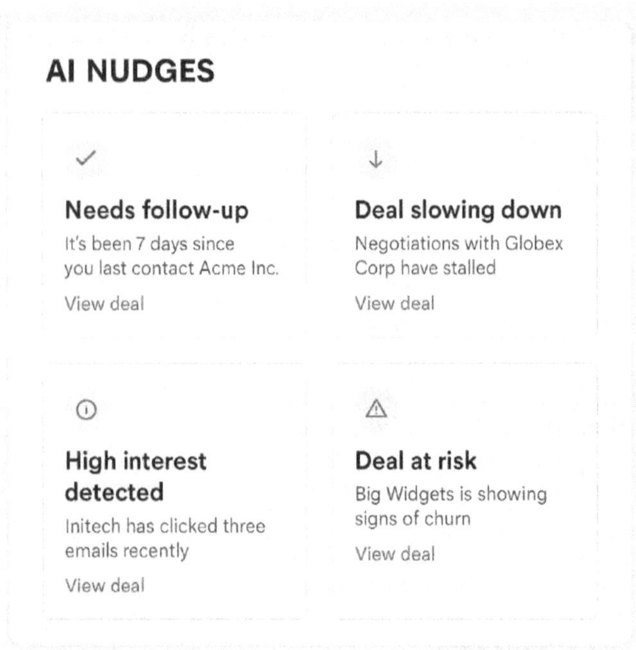

Automated Proposal and Email Generation

Speed is a closing advantage — and nothing slows a deal down like writing proposals from scratch.

With AI inside your CRM, proposal generation becomes a few-click process. Based on deal size, product interest, and buyer behavior, the system can auto-fill:

- Pricing tables
- Feature benefits relevant to the deal
- Case studies or testimonials based on the prospect's industry

CRMs like Zoho and HubSpot also offer **AI-powered email suggestions** that pull from previous interactions and templates.

Benefits:

- Faster time-to-quote
- More consistent, branded proposals
- Higher close rates with personalized messaging

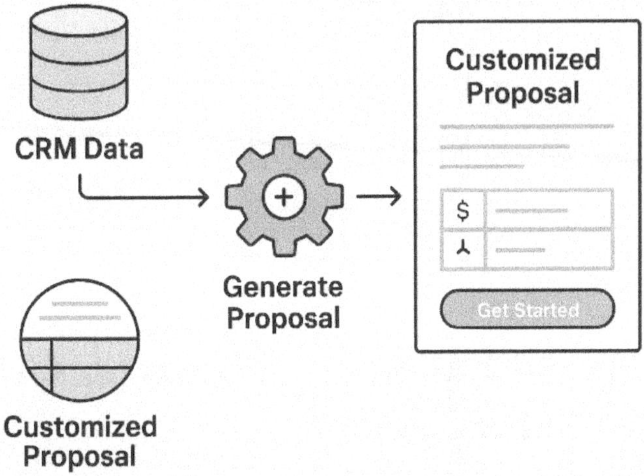

Deal-Stage Content Recommendations

Different stages of a sale need different messages. AI-enhanced CRMs now suggest the *right content* to send at the *right time* — whether it's a case study, testimonial, explainer video, or FAQ.

For example:

- Early stage → Send a one-pager overview or intro video
- Mid-stage → Offer comparison guide or case study
- Late stage → Push a testimonial, ROI calculator, or onboarding demo

This takes the guesswork out of nurturing and helps reps become trusted advisors instead of pushy sellers.

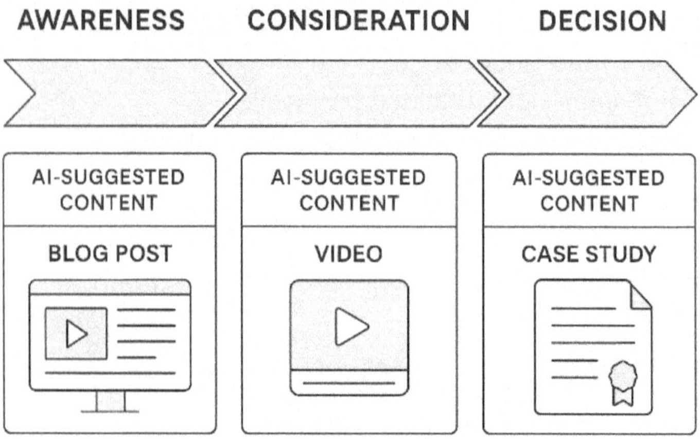

Real-World Example: A Smarter CRM, A Shorter Sales Cycle

What Happened:
A growing B2B services firm was struggling with long sales cycles and inconsistent follow-ups. They had a CRM, but it acted more like a logbook than a sales partner.

What Changed:
They switched to Pipedrive's AI features and activated smart nudges. The system started recommending when to follow up, what to send next, and flagged cold deals before they fully stalled.

The Result:
Average sales cycle time dropped by 23%. Their team booked more demos in less time, and conversion rates on quotes jumped by 18% — simply by using the right insights at the right time.

Takeaway:
With AI, your CRM isn't just a tool — it becomes a strategic teammate.

Conclusion

An AI-powered CRM turns reactive selling into *proactive closing*. Your team doesn't need more data — they need *smarter guidance*. With nudges, automated emails, and real-time proposal suggestions, even a lean team can act like a top-performing sales org.

If your CRM isn't helping you win faster — it's time to upgrade.

Next Steps

Now that your CRM is running smarter, it's time to supercharge your *sales content*. In the next chapter, we'll show you how AI can generate persuasive, on-brand messages — from live chat to full product pitches — in seconds.

Chapter 7: AI Content That Converts

Introduction

If sales is the engine of your business, content is the fuel — and AI just became your in-house copywriter, strategist, and editor.

Whether it's a sales script, FAQ, DM, or product description, today's AI tools can generate high-converting, brand-aligned content in seconds. But this isn't just about speed — it's about precision. With the right inputs, AI can write in *your* tone, reflect *your* value proposition, and adapt to different customer personas instantly.

In this chapter, we'll walk through exactly how to create AI-powered content that sells — with real examples, prompt recipes, and conversion-ready strategies any SMB can use.

Prompt Recipes for ChatGPT + Claude

A powerful AI model is only as effective as the instructions you give it. That's where *prompt recipes* come in — reusable templates that tell AI exactly what to do, how to sound, and what format to deliver.

Example Prompt:

Goal: Generate a product pitch for a wellness brand
Prompt:

"Write a 100-word product pitch for an all-natural sleep supplement. Use a friendly, knowledgeable tone. Highlight non-habit-forming ingredients and include a gentle CTA to learn more."

Prompt Types You Can Create:

- Email follow-ups
- FAQ answers
- Website product blurbs
- DM responses on social media
- Chatbot scripts for common objections

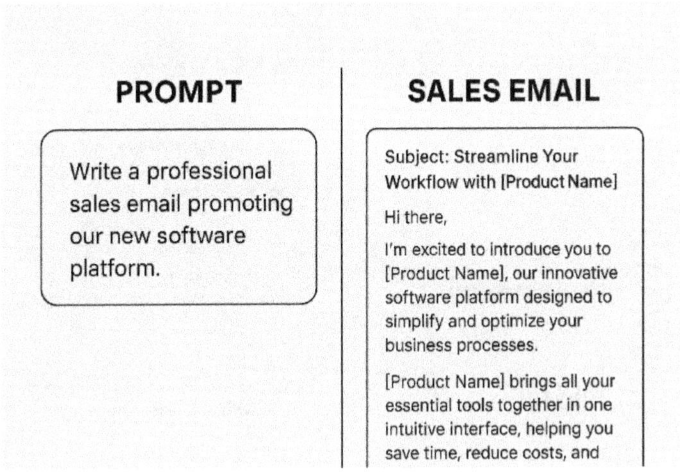

Tone-Matching to Your Brand Voice

Generic AI content won't convert — because it won't connect. That's why tone-matching is critical.

Whether your brand is warm and playful, expert and no-nonsense, or corporate and polished, AI can adapt — if you show it how.

How to Match Your Tone:

- Feed it examples of your best existing content
- Specify tone in every prompt ("Write in a friendly but confident tone")
- Refine iteratively until it reads like *you*

Tools That Help:

- **Claude (Anthropic):** Excellent at maintaining voice and context
- **ChatGPT Custom Instructions:** Allows saving tone guidance and brand style
- **Writer.com & Jasper:** Include tone-specific templates

TONE:	MESSAGE:
Friendly	Got a question? We're here to help! Reack out anytime and we'll get back to you soon.
Professional	If you have any questions, please contact us. We will respondprmptly.
Playful	Questions? Hit us up! We'll bounce back with an answer ASAP.

Real Examples Across the Funnel

Here's where AI content makes the biggest impact — the moments when speed, clarity, and relevance directly affect conversion.

Email

- **Before AI:** "Hey, just checking in…"
- **With AI:** "Hi [First Name], I noticed you explored our [Product]. Here's a short video showing how it works — and a 10% discount just for you."

Live Chat

- **Before AI:** Canned responses or slow agent replies
- **With AI:** Instant, dynamic replies based on product specs, FAQs, or competitor comparisons

DM / Social

- Personalized responses to inbound Instagram or LinkedIn messages using pre-trained brand tone and common objections

Product Pages

- SEO-optimized product descriptions generated in seconds from feature lists

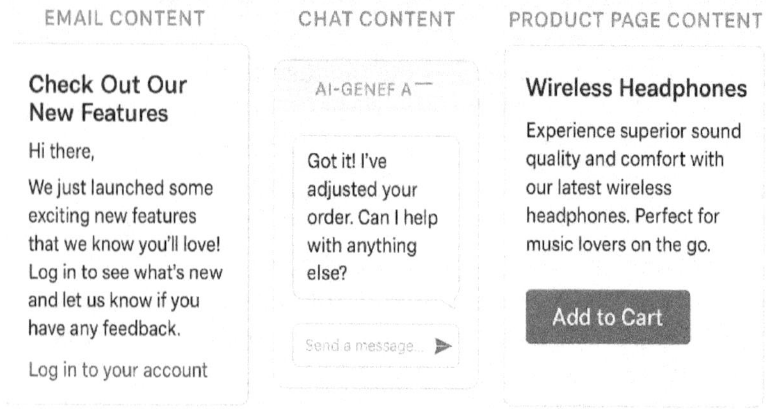

AI-Assisted Sales Objection Handling

This is where the magic happens — and where deals are won or lost.

AI can be trained to respond to common objections in real time, providing helpful, persuasive answers that convert fence-sitters into buyers.

Common Objections AI Can Handle:

- "It's too expensive."
- "I'm not sure if this is right for me."
- "I need to check with my team."
- "We already use [Competitor]."

How It Works:

- Build a prompt bank of objection-response pairs
- Train your chatbot or email templates to recognize key phrases
- Insert dynamic, helpful responses that emphasize value, proof, and urgency

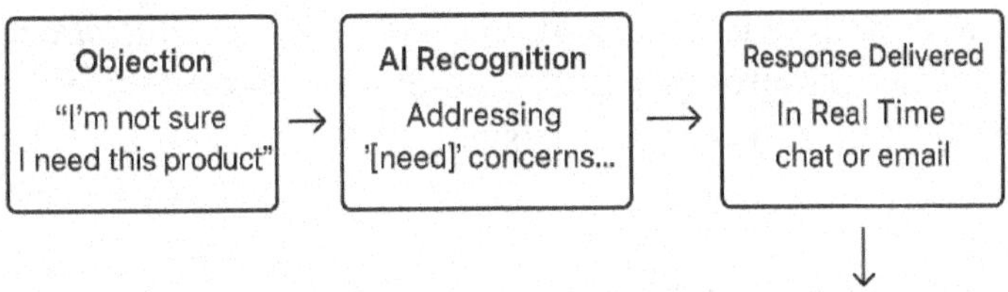

Real-World Example: From Static Pages to Dynamic Sales

What Happened:
An online home fitness brand had solid traffic but poor product page conversion. Their copy was vague and technical. They also struggled to keep up with Instagram DMs from curious shoppers.

The Fix:
They used Claude to rewrite every product description in a friendlier, more benefit-driven tone — and used ChatGPT to build a DM response bank with sales-style answers to common objections.

The Result:
Product page conversion jumped 21% within a month. DM response time dropped to 3 minutes, and weekly sales through social tripled.

Key Takeaway:
AI isn't about generic copy — it's about *smart*, contextual messaging delivered instantly. Done right, it converts.

Conclusion

AI-generated content isn't a shortcut — it's a *force multiplier*. When you match the right prompts with your brand voice and use them across the funnel, you create consistent, high-impact messaging at scale.

In today's crowded digital landscape, clarity and speed win. AI gives you both.

Next Steps

Now that you're creating content that drives action, it's time to make sure it's *measurably* working. In the next chapter, we'll break down the **metrics that matter most** — and how AI analytics can show you what's really moving the needle in support and sales.

Chapter 8: Measuring What Matters — AI Analytics for Support and Sales

Introduction

AI can automate, assist, and accelerate — but can it *prove* its impact?

For SMBs, data isn't just a dashboard feature. It's your north star for understanding where AI is driving real results and where it might be creating bottlenecks. The good news? Today's AI-powered platforms don't just perform — they *track*, *visualize*, and *interpret* what they're doing in real time.

In this chapter, we'll break down which support and sales metrics matter most, how AI-enhanced analytics bring them to life, and what to actually *do* with the insights.

Support KPIs: Know When AI Is Helping (or Hurting)

The support side of your operation is one of the richest sources of data — if you know what to look for.

AI-Enhanced Metrics to Monitor:

- **Time to First Response** – Are customers getting answers faster since automation?
- **CSAT (Customer Satisfaction Score)** – Is your AI leaving customers satisfied?
- **Resolution Rate** – Are more issues being resolved without escalation?
- **Deflection Rate** – What % of inquiries are resolved without human help?

These KPIs tell you if AI is *actually improving* customer experience — or just offloading work without delivering value.

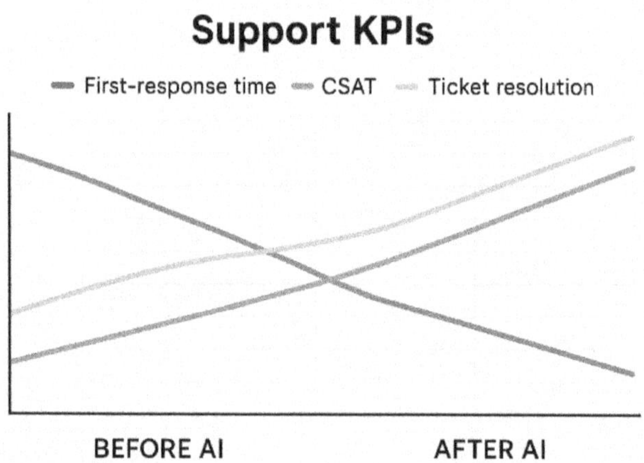

Summary:
This line graph illustrates the impact of AI implementation on key support metrics. After AI rollout, first-response time sharply decreased (blue line), while both customer satisfaction (CSAT, green line) and ticket resolution rates (yellow line) increased—highlighting measurable improvements in speed, quality, and efficiency of customer support operations.

Sales KPIs: From Gut Instinct to Data-Driven Closing

On the sales side, AI helps track *more than just activity*. It reveals intent, identifies friction points, and predicts outcomes.

Critical Sales KPIs:

- **Lead-to-Close Rate** – Are AI-scored leads converting more consistently?
- **Pipeline Velocity** – How quickly are leads moving through each stage?
- **Follow-Up Timing** – Are AI nudges improving rep response time?
- **Campaign Attribution** – Which messages or touchpoints drive conversions?

AI doesn't just collect these — it contextualizes them. You'll know *why* leads are stalling and *how* to move them forward.

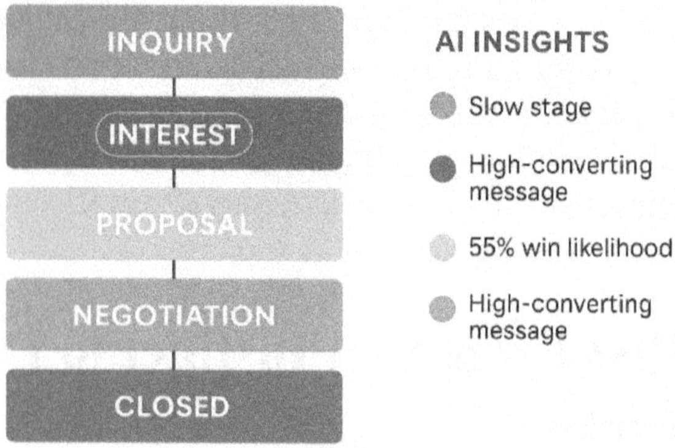

Summary:
This visual sales pipeline maps out five deal stages—from Inquiry to Closed—alongside AI-generated insights at each step. Color-coded indicators highlight where the process slows down, which messages convert best, and the predicted win rate, enabling teams to prioritize high-potential deals and streamline performance across the funnel.

Tools That Show You What AI Is Doing for You

Visibility is everything. And leading tools now come with dashboards that don't just show *outputs* — they show *impacts*.

Key Platforms Offering AI Analytics:

- **Intercom** – Tracks bot resolution rates, missed handoffs, sentiment over time
- **HubSpot** – Visualizes email engagement, lead scoring accuracy, and sales velocity
- **Zendesk AI** – Shows ticket deflection, time saved, and agent augmentation metrics
- **Zoho Zia** – Offers predictive analysis on deals and customer health

What to Look For:

- Clear separation between AI-driven and human-driven metrics
- Trendline reports (pre-AI vs. post-AI periods)
- Alerts for performance drops (e.g., CSAT declining on bot-handled tickets)

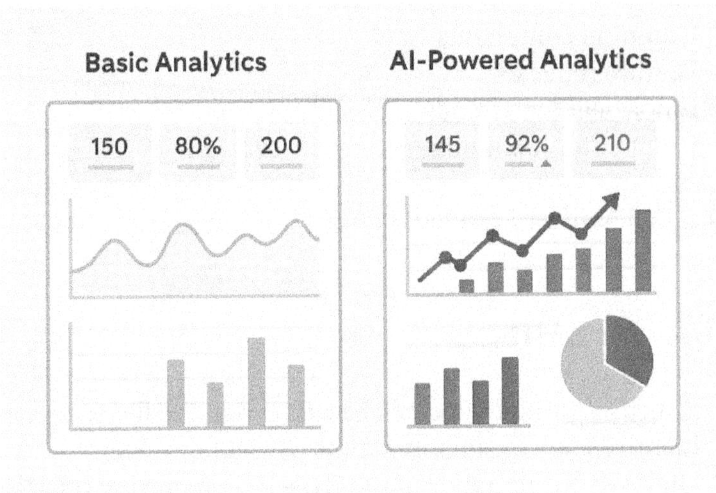

Summary:
This side-by-side comparison illustrates the difference between a basic analytics dashboard and an AI-powered one. While the basic version shows static metrics and simple graphs, the AI-enhanced dashboard highlights trends, predictions, and visual insights that help users make smarter, faster business decisions based on real-time intelligence.

Voice of the Customer Mining with AI

Sometimes, the most valuable insights come not from numbers — but from *words*.

AI-driven sentiment analysis and topic mining can comb through thousands of conversations, chats, and reviews to surface:

- Common complaints
- Feature requests
- Emotional tone trends
- Competitor mentions

This is called **Voice of the Customer (VoC) mining**, and it's a goldmine for decision-making.

Real Uses for SMBs:

- Prioritize product updates based on real feedback
- Identify gaps in support scripts or chatbot flows
- Uncover upsell opportunities based on recurring questions

AI-mined customer feedback themes

Real-World Example: What Gets Measured Gets Managed

What Happened:
A customer support platform serving real estate professionals rolled out AI to handle incoming questions. But after three months, leadership wasn't sure if it was *actually working.*

What Changed:
They implemented Zendesk's AI analytics layer. It showed that while ticket deflection was high (60%), customer satisfaction on those interactions was 40% lower than human-handled ones.

The Fix:
They refined chatbot scripts, improved tone, and adjusted escalation triggers. Within six weeks, CSAT rose by 27%, and deflection stayed high.

Lesson:
Raw performance is only half the picture. AI needs to be measured — and optimized — with the *customer* in mind.

Conclusion

Metrics matter — but only the right ones. AI analytics helps you move beyond surface-level stats to truly understand *what's working, what's not,* and how your tools are impacting both customers and revenue.

With real-time dashboards, automated insight surfacing, and clear before-and-after comparisons, even small teams can operate like data-driven pros.

Next Steps

So far, we've looked at how AI can scale, support, and sell. But now it's time to ask a deeper question: *How do we keep trust alive when machines are speaking for us?* In the next chapter, we'll explore the human side of AI — where automation meets empathy, and when it's time to hand off to humans.

Chapter 9: Human + Machine — Building Trust with AI at the Helm

Introduction

AI can automate faster than any human. But only *humans* can earn trust.

As AI becomes central to customer service and sales, the question isn't just "What can AI do?" — it's "*When should AI step aside?*" The answer lies in creating hybrid service flows that combine the speed of automation with the empathy of people.

This chapter explores how small and midsize businesses can strike the right balance — using AI to enhance human performance, not replace it. We'll cover ethical boundaries, fatigue signals, team training, and proven hybrid workflows that protect your most valuable asset: customer trust.

Ethical AI Use in Customer Conversations

When customers engage with your business, they should never feel tricked, monitored, or manipulated.

That means setting clear expectations about AI — and knowing where to draw the line.

Best Practices for Ethical Use:

- **Always disclose** when customers are interacting with a bot
- **Avoid AI-generated empathy** (e.g., "I'm sorry you're feeling that way" — unless a human is behind it)
- **Use data respectfully**, with clear opt-ins for personalization

Gray Areas to Watch:

- Using AI to simulate live chat when no humans are available
- Over-automating emotionally sensitive interactions (e.g., cancellations, complaints)
- Using behavioral data without transparency

ETHICAL	AI CUSTOMER INTERACTIONS	UNETHICAL
I am an AI assistant...	Cencare human-liike	I am just a human rep...
I'm so sorry to hear that	Error 502: Invalid input	Error 502: Invalid input
Uses data to help, not exploit	Adds users to email lists automatically	Adds users to email lists automatically
Would you like further tips?	Sends follow-ups unprompted	Sends follow-ups unprompted

Avoiding AI Fatigue and Fake Personalization

Not all automation feels helpful. When used poorly, AI becomes noise — repeating the same scripts, making clumsy assumptions, or pretending to be more "personal" than it really is.

Signs of AI Fatigue:

- Customers skipping chat prompts or asking for a human right away
- Reduced engagement with AI-generated emails
- "You don't understand me" messages in support channels

How to Avoid It:

- Rotate chatbot scripts regularly
- Limit automated touches per customer (especially during sensitive stages)
- Use personalization only when it's *context-aware*, not just name insertion

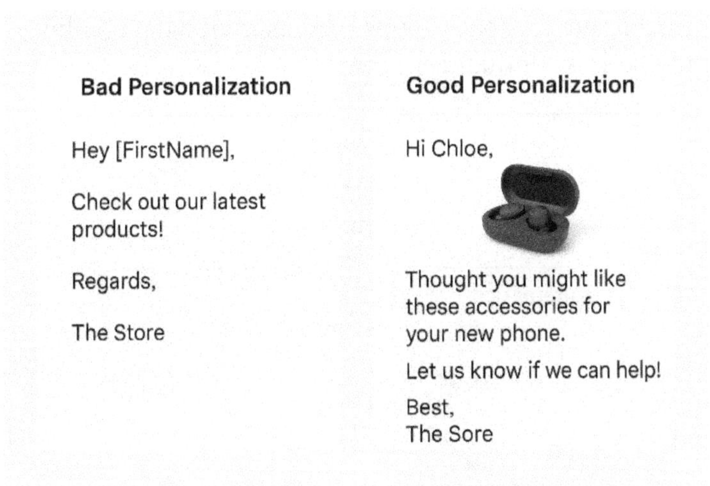

Training Support Teams to Work Alongside AI

AI tools aren't just for customers — they're for *teams*. But if your staff doesn't understand what AI is doing or when it takes over, trust can erode internally too.

Key Training Areas:

- **When AI takes over** — ticket routing, auto-replies, CRM tagging
- **When humans step in** — empathy, complex troubleshooting, decision-making
- **How to read AI cues** — sentiment scores, nudge alerts, escalation tags

Make sure your team sees AI as a teammate — not competition.

Training Tips:

- Run joint simulations (AI + human roleplay scenarios)
- Include "AI literacy" in onboarding
- Encourage feedback loops (agents reviewing chatbot transcripts for quality)

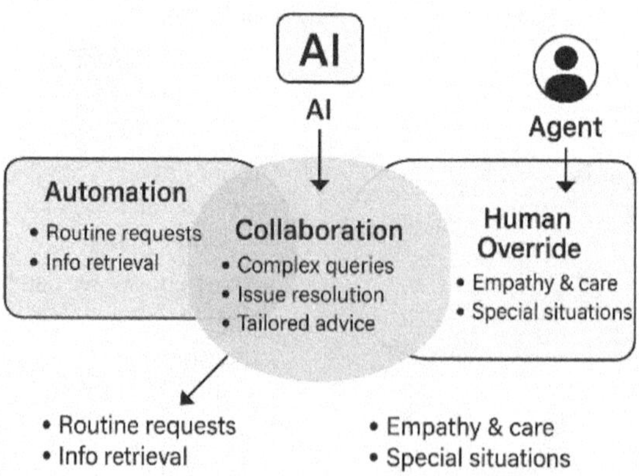

Examples of Hybrid Service Flows

The most successful SMBs don't choose between AI *or* humans — they blend both, strategically.

Example 1: Ecommerce Support

- Bot handles tracking, returns, FAQ
- Human steps in for damaged orders or refund disputes
- AI flags emotional tone for faster human routing

Example 2: B2B Sales

- AI qualifies leads via chatbot + auto-schedules a call
- Rep joins armed with AI-surfaced talking points
- AI generates follow-up email draft post-call

Example 3: SaaS Onboarding

- AI chatbot welcomes new users with a step-by-step guide
- Escalates to onboarding specialist if user skips steps or expresses confusion

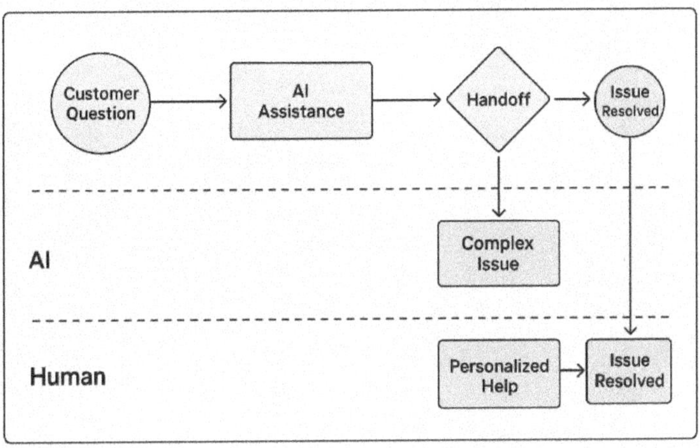

Real-World Example: The Hybrid Helpdesk That Saved the Brand

What Happened:
A popular subscription skincare brand had fully automated its support — but customer reviews tanked. People felt ignored, misunderstood, and misled when bots gave copy-paste answers to unique issues.

The Fix:
They rebuilt their support flow: AI now handles shipping, promos, and common how-tos — but hands off any sentiment-scored complaint, return request, or multi-threaded inquiry to a human. Every chatbot message now starts with a disclosure: "Hi, I'm your virtual assistant — I'll help or get someone who can."

The Results:
CSAT jumped from 62% to 91% in under 60 days. Returns were down. And customers frequently complimented the *clarity* of when they were speaking to a bot vs. a person.

Key Takeaway:
Hybrid beats automated every time — when empathy and clarity are built into the design.

Conclusion

AI can handle volume, speed, and complexity. But only *humans* can handle nuance, emotion, and trust. When you use AI to support your team — not sideline them — you create a service experience that's both scalable *and* human.

This is the future of AI for SMBs: not just faster service, but *more thoughtful* service — powered by both machine precision and human empathy.

Next Steps

You're nearly there. In the final chapter, we'll tie it all together with a 30-day action plan — a week-by-week AI blueprint to help you implement or optimize your entire support and sales stack with clarity and confidence.

Chapter 10: Your 30-Day AI Service & Sales Blueprint

Introduction

You've seen what AI can do — from automating frontline conversations to closing deals faster and analyzing results in real time. But now it's time to put all that insight into action.

Whether you're just getting started or tightening up your existing systems, this 30-day blueprint is your **step-by-step guide to launching or optimizing** your AI-powered service and sales workflow. Four weeks, four phases — each designed to help you move fast, stay focused, and deliver meaningful impact without the overwhelm.

Templates, prompts, and action steps included. Let's build your AI advantage.

Week 1: Set Up a Support Chatbot

The fastest ROI from AI often comes from automating repetitive support inquiries — and that starts with your chatbot.

What to Do:

- Choose your chatbot platform (e.g., Intercom, Tidio, Freshdesk AI)
- Import your top 20–30 FAQ entries or support ticket responses
- Set up escalation logic: when should a bot hand off to a human?
- Add clear bot disclosures: "Hi, I'm your virtual assistant!"

Tactical Tip:

Don't aim for perfection — aim for coverage. Start with the top 3–5 use cases (order tracking, returns, product questions), then refine.

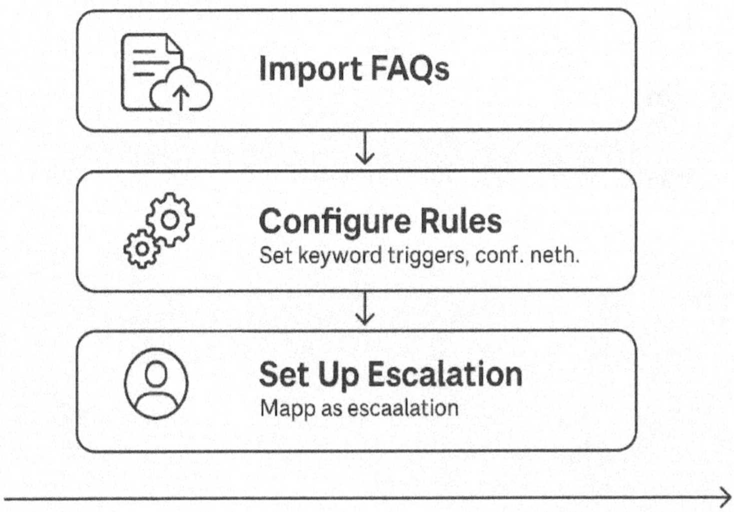

Week 2: Add Lead Capture & Email Automation

Now that your support flow is running, let's plug AI into the front of your sales funnel.

What to Do:

- Use a chatbot or website widget to collect lead data (email, interest)
- Connect with an email automation tool (HubSpot, MailerLite, ActiveCampaign)
- Set up 2–3 GPT-powered email sequences based on interest or behavior
- Pre-write follow-up prompts using your brand tone

Prompt Recipe Example:

"Write a friendly email for someone who downloaded our pricing guide but hasn't booked a call. Mention benefits of booking, include a calendar link."

Tactical Tip:

Focus on value first — what can your email *give*, not just what it wants?

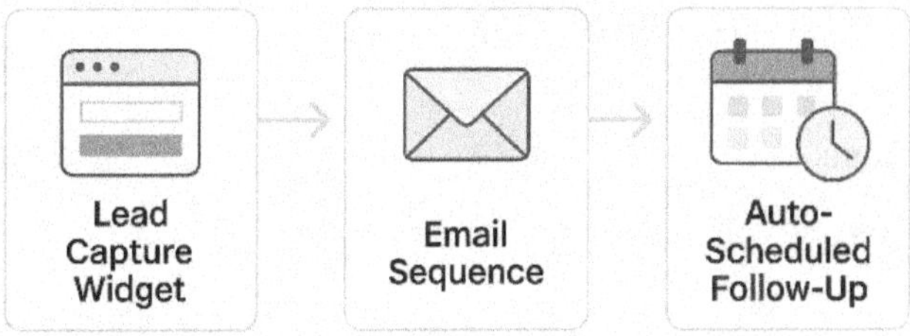

Week 3: Optimize CRM and Ticket Tagging

This week is about making your systems smarter and more connected.

What to Do:

- Review and clean up your CRM fields (remove unused tags, merge duplicates)
- Enable AI lead scoring if available (HubSpot, Zoho, Pipedrive)
- Add auto-tagging rules for incoming tickets based on keywords or sentiment
- Create smart views (e.g., “High-Intent Leads,” “Unresolved Complaints >48h”)

Tactical Tip:

Use auto-tags to drive routing. Example: "refund" + "angry sentiment" = escalate immediately.

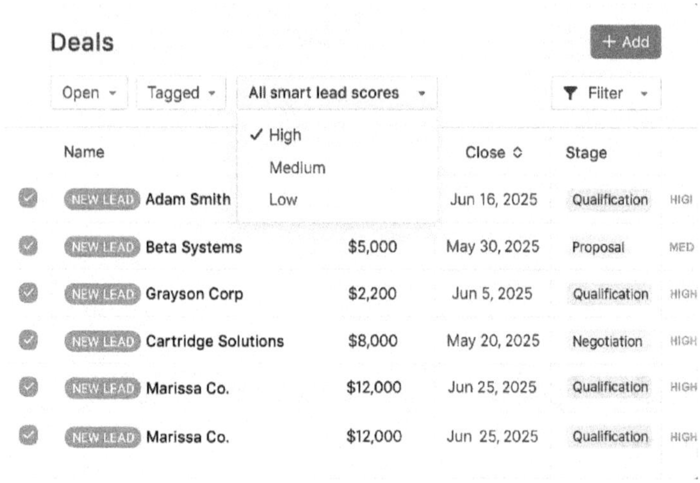

Week 4: Review KPIs and Set New AI Tasks

Now it's time to *measure what matters* — and start evolving your stack.

What to Do:

- Compare pre-AI and post-AI metrics: response time, lead velocity, conversion rate
- Identify your best-performing automations (emails, chat flows, etc.)
- Set new AI goals based on what's working: e.g., reduce missed DMs, expand chatbot to new product lines
- Schedule monthly reviews for your AI systems and data accuracy

Sample KPIs to Track:

- Support: First response time, CSAT, chatbot resolution rate
- Sales: Open rate on AI-written emails, bookings from chatbot, lead-to-close ratio

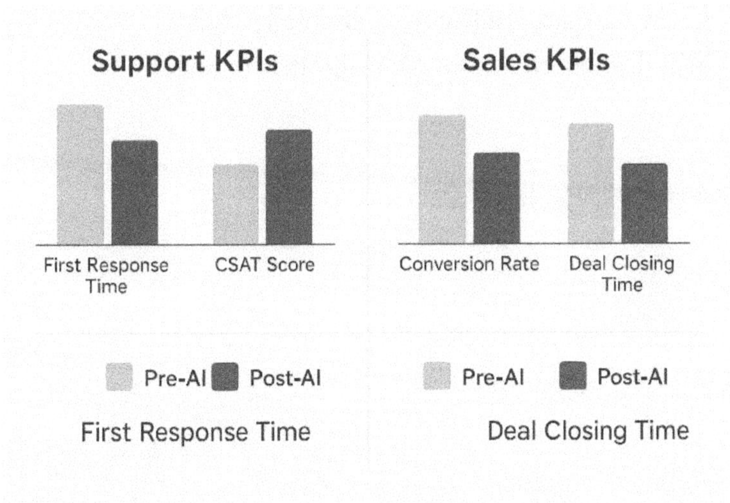

Templates, Prompts, and Checklist

Here's your plug-and-play toolkit to launch faster:

Email Follow-Up Prompt:

"Write a warm follow-up email to someone who visited our pricing page but didn't convert. Mention our 30-day guarantee and include a calendar link."

Chatbot Response Prompt:

"Create a chatbot reply for: 'I want to return my item.' Make it friendly, direct, and include a link to the return policy."

Weekly Checklist:

Week	Key Deliverables
1	Chatbot live, FAQ imported, escalation tested
2	Lead form active, email automation running
3	CRM tags set, lead scoring enabled
4	KPI dashboard reviewed, insights acted on

4-WEEK AI CHECKLIST

	WEEK 1	WEEK 2	WEEK 3	WEEK 4
SUPPORT	☐			
SALES	☐			
CRM	☐			
REVIEW	☐			
	☐			
	☐			

Real-World Example: From Chaos to Clarity in 30 Days

What Happened:
A solo founder running an online coaching business was overwhelmed by support emails, missed leads, and inconsistent follow-up. Every task felt urgent — and none felt scalable.

What Changed:
Over four weeks, she followed a simplified version of this blueprint:

- Set up a Tidio chatbot for pre-sales questions
- Used ChatGPT to generate a 3-part email sequence for new subscribers
- Integrated HubSpot's free CRM with tagging and lead scoring
- Reviewed support data weekly to adjust chatbot scripts

The Result:
Her average response time dropped by 85%. Email open rates climbed to 42%. Most importantly, she went from *reactive scrambling* to *strategic execution* — with room to grow.

Conclusion

You don't need to "figure out AI" — you just need to *get started.*

This 30-day plan gives you the momentum, clarity, and structure to launch or optimize AI in your support and sales workflow. Think of it not as a tech overhaul — but as a capacity upgrade for your existing team.

In a month, you'll be faster, smarter, and more scalable. And that's just the beginning.

CHECK YOUR BONUS AT THE END !

AI-Powered Customer Service & Sales: Glossary of Terms

AI (Artificial Intelligence)

Software systems that mimic human thinking to perform tasks like answering questions, analyzing behavior, and making recommendations. In sales and support, AI helps automate, predict, and personalize at scale.

Automation

The use of technology to perform tasks without human intervention. In this book, automation includes chatbots responding to FAQs, email sequences triggered by lead actions, and CRM tagging based on keywords.

Auto-Routing

An AI feature that analyzes incoming support or sales requests and automatically directs them to the most appropriate team or individual, reducing delays and miscommunication.

Bot / Chatbot

An AI-powered virtual assistant that handles customer conversations. Bots can answer questions, collect leads, schedule meetings, or escalate issues to humans when needed.

Calendar Booking Flow

A feature where AI automatically schedules meetings with leads or clients based on their preferences and your availability, often integrated with platforms like Calendly or HubSpot Meetings.

ChatGPT

An advanced AI language model developed by OpenAI. Used to generate natural-sounding content for emails, chats, product pages, and customer interactions.

Claude

A conversational AI model developed by Anthropic, known for its ability to maintain tone and long-form context. Useful for personalized brand-aligned messaging and chatbot workflows.

CRM (Customer Relationship Management)

A system used to store and manage customer data, track interactions, and guide sales efforts. AI-enhanced CRMs (like HubSpot, Zoho, Pipedrive) help automate insights, lead scoring, and follow-ups.

CSAT (Customer Satisfaction Score)

A key support metric that reflects how satisfied customers are with a recent interaction. Often measured via post-chat or post-ticket surveys.

Deflection Rate

The percentage of support tickets resolved by AI or self-service tools without involving a human agent. High deflection = more efficient support.

Email Automation

Pre-scheduled, behavior-triggered email campaigns designed to nurture leads, follow up on actions, or reactivate interest — powered by tools like MailerLite, ActiveCampaign, or HubSpot.

Escalation

The process where a bot or automated system hands off a conversation to a human agent — usually triggered by frustration signals, failed responses, or complexity.

FAQ Pre-Training

Training an AI chatbot using your company's actual frequently asked questions, product details, and previous support logs — to improve accuracy and reduce confusion.

First Response Time

A key performance metric showing how quickly a customer receives an initial reply — often dramatically improved with AI-powered bots and automation.

GPT-Powered Emails

Email content generated by large language models like ChatGPT. These emails are tone-optimized, personalized, and often used for follow-ups, outreach, or re-engagement.

Hybrid Service Flow

A system where both AI and humans work together — AI handles predictable or repetitive tasks, while humans step in for complex, emotional, or high-stakes conversations.

Intercom

A customer messaging platform combining live chat, AI bots, and ticketing, used widely for support and proactive sales engagement.

KPI (Key Performance Indicator)

Quantifiable metrics used to track performance. In AI service and sales, common KPIs include response time, CSAT, conversion rate, and pipeline velocity.

Lead Scoring

An AI-driven process that ranks sales leads based on engagement, behavior, and likelihood to convert — helping prioritize the most valuable prospects.

Live Chat

A real-time messaging tool on websites or apps. Often supported by bots for initial handling, then passed to human agents when needed.

Nudge

A small AI-generated prompt, alert, or suggestion that guides a salesperson or support agent to act — such as "This deal is stalling" or "Follow up with this lead."

Pipeline Velocity

A sales KPI that tracks how quickly leads move through each stage of the sales process. AI can help increase velocity by suggesting next actions and removing friction.

Predictive Insights

AI-generated observations based on patterns in your CRM, emails, or customer behavior — used to forecast outcomes or recommend the next best step.

Proposal Automation

Using AI and CRM data to auto-generate sales proposals — often including pricing, timelines, and benefits — saving time and improving consistency.

Prompt Recipe

A reusable instruction or input you give to an AI tool (like ChatGPT or Claude) to generate specific content, such as a sales script, product description, or chatbot message.

Sentiment Analysis

AI's ability to interpret emotional tone from text or speech — e.g., identifying if a customer is frustrated, confused, or satisfied — and acting accordingly.

Smart Tagging

Automatic labeling of CRM records or support tickets based on content, keywords, or tone. Helps segment contacts and route tasks intelligently.

Support Deflection

When AI successfully answers a customer's question or solves a problem *without* needing a human, reducing workload for your support team.

Tidio

An all-in-one live chat and AI chatbot tool, popular among e-commerce SMBs for its ease of setup and multilingual capabilities.

Ticket Resolution Rate

A support KPI tracking how many customer issues are fully resolved — whether by human or bot — and used to measure team or tool effectiveness.

Tone-Matching

The process of aligning AI-generated content with your brand voice — whether formal, casual, friendly, or expert — to maintain consistency across messages.

Voice Assistant Integration

AI-powered systems (like Alexa or Google Assistant) that let customers use voice commands to interact with your service, check orders, or get support — often integrated into support systems.

Voice of Customer (VoC) Mining

Using AI to analyze customer reviews, chats, surveys, and tickets to identify patterns, pain points, and opportunities. Helps inform product development, marketing, and service improvements.

Bonus – FREE eBook Version

Want the full-color PDF version of this book?
Simply email me at **ericl@acrasolution.com** with a **screenshot of your Amazon purchase and positive review**, and I'll gladly send you your personal copy.

Thank you for taking the time to read this eBook.

Your support means more than you know. **By purchasing this book, you're directly contributing to the creation of more high-quality, practical resources** for business owners, IT leaders, and everyday professionals navigating the complex world of cybersecurity. It's because of readers like you that I can continue researching, writing, and delivering tools that make a real difference.

Whether you leave a positive review, recommend this book to a colleague, or simply apply what you've learned — **you're helping grow a stronger, safer business community. And for that, I sincerely thank you.**

At **AcraSolution**, we're committed to providing both premium services and a wide range of **free, actionable tools**. Our growing library includes documentation, articles, and step-by-step guides — designed to bring you immediate value, no strings attached.

If you need additional guidance or support, don't hesitate to visit our website www.acrasolution.com or reach out directly.

Together, we can build a more secure future.

— Eric LeBouthillier
Author & Cybersecurity Strategist

www.ingramcontent.com/pod-product-compliance
Lightning Source LLC
LaVergne TN
LVHW010349250925
821895LV00023B/201
9781997754008